Amphibians

CHRISTINE TAYLOR-BUTLER

Children's Press®
An Imprint of Scholastic Inc.
New York Toronto London Auckland Sydney
Mexico City New Delhi Hong Kong
Danbury, Connecticut

Content Consultant
Stephen S. Ditchkoff, PhD
Professor of Wildlife Sciences
Auburn University
Auburn, Alabama

Library of Congress Cataloging-in-Publication Data
Taylor-Butler, Christine.
  Amphibians / by Christine Taylor-Butler.
    pages cm—(A true book)
  Audience: Ages 9-12.
  Audience: Grades 4 to 6.
  Includes bibliographical references and index.
  ISBN 978-0-531-21750-4 (lib. bdg.) — ISBN 978-0-531-22335-2 (pbk.)
  1. Amphibians—Juvenile literature. I. Title.
  QL644.2.T33 2014
  597.8—dc23   2013000097

All rights reserved. Published in 2014 by Children's Press, an imprint of Scholastic Inc.
Printed in China 62
SCHOLASTIC, CHILDREN'S PRESS, A TRUE BOOK ™, and associated logos are trademarks and/or registered trademarks of Scholastic Inc.
1 2 3 4 5 6 7 8 9 10 R 23 22 21 20 19 18 17 16 15 14

Front cover: A frog eating a grasshopper
Back cover: Newt swimming underwater

Find the Truth!

Everything you are about to read is true **except** for one of the sentences on this page.

Which one is **TRUE**?

T or F Some salamanders breathe through their skin.

T or F Caecilians are the largest worms in the world.

Find the answers in this book.

Contents

THE **BIG** TRUTH!

A frog leaps to catch a tasty insect.

4 Life Cycle

5 Endangered Species

Some caecilians spend their entire lives in water.

CHAPTER 1

Predators Below Us

In a tropical forest near the Amazon River, a small creature clings to the bark of a tree. Its bulging red eyes blink in the dark. The four sticky toes on each of its four webbed feet keep the red-eyed tree frog tightly in place. Its sticky tongue lashes toward an insect that wanders by. In an instant, the frog snares its prey and swallows the insect with one gulp. Then it lies in wait for another.

A group of red-eyed tree frogs is called an army.

A Giant in the River

An 80-pound (36.3-kilogram) Japanese giant salamander burrows into a riverbank and waits until nightfall. Then it slips into the water to begin its journey. Unlike its 6-inch (15.2-centimeter) relatives, this animal grows longer than 5 feet (1.5 meters). Like salmon, it swims upstream to lay its eggs. Nodes, or special bumps, on its body help it detect prey. The skeleton of this animal is very close to that of its dinosaur relatives. Scientists call it a "living fossil."

Japanese giant salamanders live up to 80 years.

Caecilians thrive in the wet and warm tropical climate.

Burrowing Hunter

Deep beneath the ground, a caecilian inches along a series of dark tunnels. This snakelike predator's muscles contract and expand as it moves. Because its tiny eyes are buried beneath folds of skin, it uses tentacles to detect the scent of prey. Soon a small worm crosses its path. The predator strikes, catching the worm in its strong jaws.

These three animals have something in common. Can you guess what that is?

A frog sits partially
submerged in a lake.

CHAPTER 2

It's Classified

These animals are all amphibians. But what exactly is an amphibian? The word *amphibian* comes from the Greek word *amphibios*, which means "living a double life." Most amphibians live part of their lives in water and part on the land. They are cold-blooded vertebrates. As vertebrates, they have a backbone. But because they are cold-blooded, their bodies can't generate heat. As a result, they need a warm environment to survive.

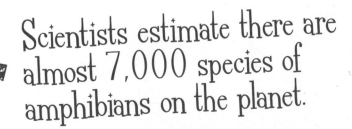

Scientists estimate there are almost 7,000 species of amphibians on the planet.

Understanding Amphibians

Scientists use a system of **classification** to keep track of animal species. It is similar to a family tree. **Class** describes amphibians' main category, Amphibia. Subclass breaks amphibians into periods in time. There are three subclasses of amphibians. Two subclasses existed thousands of years ago and are now extinct. The third, called Lissamphibia, contains the amphibians we see today.

Modern amphibians are broken into three groups called orders: **Anura**, **Caudata**, and **Gymnophiona**.

Scientists have found fossils of amphibians dating back hundreds of millions of years.

Scientists believe that amphibians have existed for around 360 million years.

Quick Facts About Amphibians

Group (number of species)	Diet	Reproduction	Distribution	Life Span
Frogs and Toads (6,000)	Carnivorous, eating insects, worms, slugs, rodents, other reptiles	All lay eggs	Found on every continent except Antarctica	2–40 years, depending on species
Salamanders and Newts (More than 600)	Carnivorous, eating insects, worms, grubs, mollusks, small rodents, fish, frogs	Almost all lay eggs; the fire salamander bears live young	Found on every continent except Australia and Antarctica	10–55 years, depending on species
Caecilians (More than 180)	Carnivorous, eating worms, termites, frogs, lizards	Most species bear live young; an estimated 25 percent lay eggs	Most are found in wet, tropical regions of Central and South America, Asia, and Africa	Up to 13 years in zoos; unknown in the wild

A cave salamander rests on a rock.

13

To leap, frogs coil their tendons like springs before launching themselves into the air.

Frogs and Toads

The order Anura contains frogs and toads. *Anura* is a Greek word meaning "without a tail." Frogs and toads lose their tails when they become adults. There are about 6,000 species.

Frogs have smooth skin and long back legs for jumping. Their skin is moist, and some have special pads on their webbed toes that help them climb trees. They have upper teeth but not lower teeth.

Toads are a particular type of frog. Toads have drier skin and shorter legs than other frogs. Their bodies are heavier. You can often tell a toad by the bumps on its body. It can't hop very far, and it has no teeth.

Frogs and toads come in a variety of colors that help them survive. A dull color helps them blend in with their environment. A bright color might signal that the skin secretes, or produces, poisons.

A person cannot get warts from toads.

Salamanders and Newts

The order Caudata contains salamanders and newts. *Caudata* is a Latin word meaning "tail." These amphibians keep their tails when they become adults. There are more than 600 species.

Most salamanders are less than 6 inches (15.2 cm) long and have smooth skin. However, the Chinese giant salamander grows as long as 6 feet (1.8 m). It may weigh up to 140 pounds (63.5 kg). Their back legs grow slower than their front legs.

A fire salamander hunts for a meal.

Salamander is Greek for "fire lizard."

Some salamanders and newts, such as this eastern newt, are brightly colored.

Unlike frogs and toads, most adult salamanders have no lungs or gills for breathing. They absorb oxygen through their skin and through membranes in their mouths. However, in nature there are often exceptions to the rule. For example, siren salamanders never lose the gills they had at birth. Tiger salamanders develop lungs as adults.

Newts are also salamanders. But they have dry, often bumpy skin. Newts spend more time in the water than other salamanders.

The rings on a caecilian's body are actually folds of skin.

Caecilians

Caecilians belong to the order Gymnophiona. *Gymnophiona* is Greek for "naked serpent." A caecilian has no legs or feet and looks like a giant worm. But don't be fooled. Its teeth are huge for its size, and it has tentacles and thick, shiny skin. Caecilians live in networks of underground tunnels. Because they are in the dark, caecilians' tiny, rarely used eyes are sometimes hidden. Like most amphibians, their gills become lungs at adulthood. There are more than 180 species of caecilians.

Alien Invaders

One hundred cane toads were brought to Australia in 1935 to control beetles that were destroying local sugarcane crops. Though they helped solve this problem, they caused many more. Because female cane toads can lay thousand of eggs, the toads quickly multiplied. They attacked the insect populations, and ate birds' eggs and frogs. A cane toad's skin produces a powerful poison that kills any predator, making it difficult to remove them. There are now millions of cane toads in Australia.

CHAPTER 3

Habitats

Amphibians live everywhere except in the coldest
climates. They need a moist habitat to keep their
skin from drying out and to lay their eggs. You'll

World Distribution of Amphibians

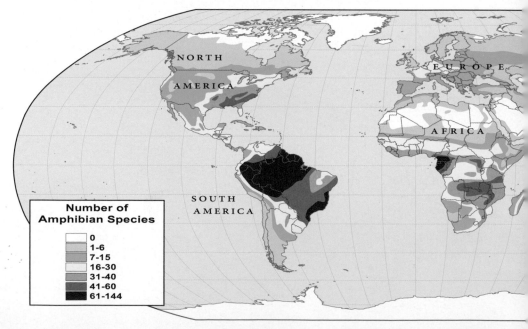

often find them near lakes, marshes, or ponds in your backyard. Because they are cold-blooded, amphibians need the sun or warm surroundings to heat their bodies. In hot climates, they burrow underground or stay in the water to cool off. In colder climates, some amphibians hibernate during winter.

The world's smallest frog was discovered in Papua New Guinea.

Finding a Home

Frogs and toads have the greatest number of species among amphibians. On average, they live about seven years. They thrive in many habitats, from marshes and bogs to farmland and mountains. You'll find frogs in trees in the Amazon or under leaves on the forest floor.

Habitat loss is a big problem for frogs. As more cities and towns are built, water is diverted from wetlands. Roads are a hazard to frogs trying to reach breeding grounds.

Many tropical frogs, including poison dart frogs like this one, are facing extinction.

Frogs help control the insect population.

Versatile Abilities

Frogs can travel long distances because of their strong legs. They can hop four times their body length. Some can use their legs to burrow into the ground to hibernate.

Frogs have good eyesight and can spot prey easily. Most eat insects, worms, and slugs. Some eat rodents and reptiles.

Frogs and toads are the only amphibians that make a sound. Have you heard male frogs croaking at night? They do this to attract a mate.

Great crested newts are most often found in bodies of freshwater in Europe.

Salamander Habits and Habitats

Salamanders and newts are found on every continent except Australia and Antarctica. One-third of all known species are found in North America.

Some salamanders are aquatic. They remain in the water for most of their lives. Most salamanders live in shady areas near ponds and lakes or in caves. They are normally nocturnal. During the day, they sleep under rocks or inside logs. At night, they come out of hiding to find food.

Salamanders don't have ears, but they can see or smell their prey. They can also sense vibrations. All salamanders are carnivorous, which means they eat meat. Insects such as crickets, fruit flies, and termites have been found in their stomachs. They also eat worms, grubs, and mollusks. Larger salamanders can eat small rodents, fish, and frogs. In a protected environment, salamanders can live 20 years or even longer, depending on the species.

A Strinati's cave salamander hunts a mosquito in a cave in Italy.

Hidden Amphibians

Caecilians are found in the wet, tropical regions of Central and South America, Africa, and Asia. Not much is known about these mysterious creatures because they live underground or in water. What is known is that they range in length from 3.5 inches (8.9 cm) to almost 5 feet (1.5 m).

Although caecilians look like giant worms, they have a bony skeleton. Their hard-pointed skulls make it easy for them to tunnel through the dirt.

Caecilians spend most of their lives underground or underwater.

A caecilian's tentacles are retractable, much like a cat's claws.

A Rio Cauca caecilian absorbs most of the oxygen it needs through its skin.

Caecilians have tiny eyes and no ears. They use tentacles near their eyes to detect prey. When something comes near, they can use their strong jaws and sharp teeth to grab it. Caecilians eat mostly worms and termites. Some also eat frogs, lizards, and sometimes other caecilians. They don't chew their food, but swallow it whole. Like other amphibians, they excrete a toxin to protect themselves from being eaten by other predators.

Frog Early Warning System

Dr. Tyrone Hayes has loved frogs all his life. Now his research has led to a startling discovery. Atrazine, a common farm pesticide, causes genetic deformities in tadpoles and adult frogs. The pesticide leaks into the ground and water supplies and is absorbed through a frog's thin skin.

Sixty million pounds (27.2 million kg) of atrazine is used in the United States each year.

Dr. Hayes's discovery showed that pesticides alter tadpoles at the cellular level. The amount of pesticide that harmed the frogs he studied was less than what is allowed in human drinking water. Now Dr. Hayes warns there may be risks to humans, too.

CHAPTER 4

Life Cycle

Scientists believe that amphibians first developed around 360 million years ago, when sea creatures began to adapt to the land. Amphibians can still exist in both places. That is why they are usually found near sources of water.

Amphibians go through a process called **metamorphosis**. This means their bodies make a drastic change from juvenile stage to adult stage. They are the only vertebrates in the animal kingdom that undergo this process.

Green algae growing in salamander eggs help the salamanders grow healthy.

Dramatic Development

Frogs and toads undergo the most dramatic change. The female lays unfertilized eggs in water or on a leaf filled with dew. She may lay thousands of them. Unlike reptile eggs, which have a hard shell, amphibian eggs are surrounded by a jellylike substance. The collection of eggs is called a **clutch** and must be fertilized by a male to begin growing.

The fertilized eggs hatch into babies called tadpoles. They have gills that allow them to breathe underwater and a tail to help them swim.

Metamorphosis can last several months. By 6 weeks, a tadpole's lungs form and its gills disappear. Back legs form at 8 weeks. At 12 weeks, its front legs form and the tail begins to disappear. Soon the frog is ready to live on land. The juvenile frog then takes years to become an adult.

Life Cycle: From Tadpole to Frog

A female frog lays eggs near the bank of a river. A male fertilizes them.

Tadpoles hatch with gills and a tail. They have no legs.

Adult frogs are fully developed and can live on land.

Back legs develop, and the tadpoles' tails begin to shrink.

The tadpoles develop front legs and feet. Gills have disappeared, and lungs have developed.

Spectacled salamanders lay groups of eggs underwater.

Not all salamanders give birth the same way. Some species lay their eggs in water, just as frogs and toads do. Others lay their eggs on land. Young salamanders are called **larvae** or **efts**.

Unlike frogs, salamanders and newts keep their tails when they become adults. Many also keep their gills. The North American mud puppy is one example. This salamander can continue to live in the water as an adult.

Lungless salamanders are an exception to the rule. Their young do not go through metamorphosis. They are fully formed when they hatch. These amphibians are called **direct developers**.

Fire salamanders are the only amphibians that undergo live birth. They hatch while still inside the mother's body and then are deposited in the water. But don't touch them! Their brightly colored skin contains a dangerous poison.

Lungless salamanders, such as the seepage salamander, look like smaller versions of their parents when they hatch.

35

Caecilians have two different life cycles, depending on the species. Some species give birth to fully developed babies. Others lay their eggs in water. When the eggs hatch, the larvae eat algae and plankton for nourishment. They use their small tails to help them swim. The larvae go through metamorphosis to become adults. They lose their gills and develop one lung for breathing. Their skin becomes thick, the tail disappears, and tentacles form near their eyes.

A scientist holds a three-week-old Gaboon caecilian.

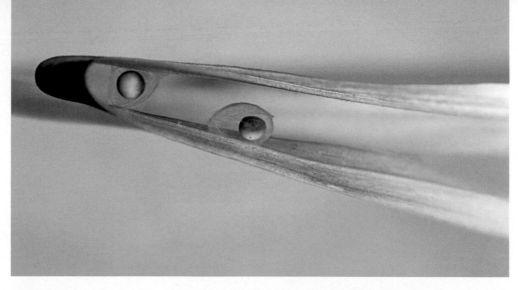

These two newt eggs were wrapped protectively in the leaf of an underwater plant.

Good Parenting?

Lungless salamanders curl around their eggs to keep them warm. Both parents protect the eggs. Some newts wrap each egg in a leaf to protect it from predators. Caecilian females sometimes shed their skin for their babies to eat. The skin is filled with nutrients.

Frogs, on the other hand, often abandon their eggs. However, a species of poison dart frogs in South America is an exception. The males hug the clutch and then carry the hatched young to the water.

A scientist measures a frog she captured in the wild for study.

CHAPTER 5

Endangered Species

Amphibians are in danger. More than 60 percent of the species are in decline. One hundred twenty species have become extinct since 1980. Habitat loss is one reason for their disappearance.

Because amphibians absorb moisture through their skin, they are sensitive to toxins in their environment. These include fungi, bacteria, and chemicals in the water and soil. Scientists believe the declining health of amphibians indicates the human population is at risk as well.

← Herpetologists study both reptiles and amphibians. Batrachologists study only amphibians.

Medical Marvels

The study of amphibians has led to important breakthroughs in medical research. Some scientists study chemicals secreted by frogs. Samples taken from three frog species have shown that the secretions can block the spread of HIV, a dangerous disease. The secretions of poison dart frogs are 200 times more powerful at blocking pain than morphine, a drug used to treat severe pain. Experts have also had medical breakthroughs for frogs. One scientist discovered a way to protect frogs against a certain disease.

Chemicals secreted by giant leaf frogs can help lessen pain and fight certain illnesses in people.

The El Valle Amphibian Conservation Center in Panama works to protect at-risk amphibian species from extinction.

Supporting Threatened Species

Organizations are springing into action to save the amphibian population. Scientists at the University of California, Berkeley, created the AmphibiaWeb project. This Web site allows experts to upload their research on amphibians. The site has cataloged 7,000 species so far.

The Global Amphibian Assessment project trains specialists, funds expeditions, and creates protected areas for wildlife. There are many other groups involved in the fight, including the Amphibian Conservation Program run by the Smithsonian National Zoo.

Amphibians are extremely sensitive to changes in their environment.

In fact, zoos across the country have joined together to educate the public. They also breed species in captivity that can be released into the wild. Experts hope the released animals can repopulate declining species.

Many people work to protect amphibian habitats. This includes slowing the destruction of forests, streams, and wetlands, and reducing toxic chemicals in our environment. The environmental changes that threaten amphibians also affect us. Protecting amphibians is protecting humans, too.

A Deadly Fungus

A fungal disease called chytrid is killing frogs at an alarming rate. Dr. Vance Vredenburg (below) knew that a type of bacteria destroys the chytrid fungus. Vredenburg caught 100 frogs. Eighty were bathed in the bacteria and tagged. Twenty were simply tagged. All 100 frogs were released. Two months later, Vredenburg discovered that the frogs exposed to the bacteria were better able to resist chytrid. Now Vredenburg and other scientists are studying to see if the bacteria can help save frogs on a wider scale. ★

True Statistics

Smallest amphibian in the world: *Paedophryne amauensis* (a frog), 0.25 in. (0.6 cm)

Largest amphibian in the world: Giant Chinese salamander, 6 ft. (1.8 m)

Second-smallest frog in the world: Brazilian gold frog, 0.4 in. (1 cm)

Smallest toad in the world: Flea toad, 0.4 in. (1 cm)

Largest frog in the world: Goliath frog, 1 ft. (0.3 m), 6.5 lb (2.9 kg)

Largest caecilian in the world: *Caecilia thompsoni*, 5 ft. (1.5 m)

Smallest caecilian in the world: *Grandisonia brevis*, 4.5 in. (11.4 cm)

Smallest salamander in the world: *Thorius arboreus*, 0.6 in. (1.5 cm)

Did you find the truth?

(T) Some salamanders breathe through their skin.

(F) Caecilians are the largest worms in the world.

Resources

Books

Berger, Melvin, and Gilda Berger. *Amphibians*. New York: Scholastic, 2011.

Pringle, Laurence, and Meryl Henderson. *Frogs! Strange and Wonderful*. Honesdale, PA: Boyds Mills, 2012.

Turner, Pamela S., and Andy Comins. *The Frog Scientist*. Boston: Houghton Mifflin Books for Children, 2009.

Visit this Scholastic Web site for more information on amphibians:

★ www.factsfornow.scholastic.com
Enter the keyword **Amphibians**

Important Words

Anura (uh-NYUR-uh) — the order of amphibians that includes frogs and toads

Caudata (kow-DAH-tuh) — the order of amphibians that includes salamanders and newts

class (KLAS) — a group of related plants or animals that is larger than an order but smaller than a phylum

classification (klas-uh-fuh-KAY-shuhn) — the separation of things into groups according to the characteristics that they have in common

clutch (KLUHCH) — a nest of eggs

direct developers (duh-REKT duh-VEL-up-urz) — animals whose young are born looking similar to adults of the species

efts (EFTS) — young newts that live on land before returning to the water when they become adults

Gymnophiona (jihm-noh-FEE-oh-nuh) — the order of amphibians that includes caecilians

larvae (LAHR-vee) — newly hatched amphibians

metamorphosis (met-uh-MOR-fuh-sis) — a series of changes some animals go through as they develop into adults

Index

Page numbers in **bold** indicate illustrations

About the Author

Christine Taylor-Butler is the author of more than 60 books for children, including the True Book series on American History/Government, Health and the Human Body, and Science Experiments. A graduate of the Massachusetts Institute of Technology, Christine holds degrees in both civil engineering and art and design. She currently lives in Kansas City, Missouri.